Design Unveiled: A Beginner's Guide to the Art of Graphic Design

Discovering the Core Principles Behind Every Design Project

Contents

Is This Book for You?

Do you need to design things, but have no background in graphic design theory? Are you a starting blogger, small business owner or a zero-budget marketing specialist who needs to create content for social media, advertisements, brochures or images for a web page? Do you want to learn the main graphic design principles to create visuals that effectively communicate your message?

If you lack a degree in art but need to make social media posts, simple ads, business cards, flyers, web visuals, brochures or any other visuals, buy this book and read it. It won't substitute studying in a design school, but it will give you a vocabulary of the basic design and composition principles, color theory, and typography in a quick and practical way. This book ideally serves as a good starting point, if you want to learn how to produce better-designed visuals and never again make amateur mistakes. Moreover, after reading it you will know exactly why your designs look better than they were before.

The idea of this book is not just telling you theoretical principles about using colors, creating compositional balance and pairing typefaces correctly, but to show you how you can apply these principles in the real world to improve your design. You will be educated enough to understand when the design created really helps to communicate your message and when it doesn't.

In order to make this book as practical as possible, you will see illustrations and examples of every principle that is described as well as **will learn about the free online resources** you can use for creating your new designs. Recommended especially for non-designers this book will change the way you look at graphic designs around you.

Read this book and you will learn how to:
- use the main principles of professionally looking designs
- create a composition and use visual weight, balance, and flow, in order to emphasize your message,
- recognize the difference between the optical and geographic center and why the first one is important.
- use the science behind the good looking color schemes
- combine typefaces and use contrast in a sophisticated way,
- use more than 20 FREE resources for creating your own designs.

In short, after reading this book you will know how to apply the same design principles every professional designer knows and uses.

CRAP – The Big Four

Apple Co-founder Steve Jobs once said: "Design is not just what it looks like and feels like. Design is how it works." A common misconception is that design is only about the way a product, advertisement, web page etc. *looks.* In reality, a purpose of a good design is to make sure that the design *works and communicates.* It must help to sell a product or communicate a message.

Have you ever bought a product or a service simply because its packaging or website *looked* nicer than the alternative? Nothing big, just perhaps a shampoo that has a nicer packaging, or an online course that has more professionally designed advertisement. When you need to choose between products with similar prices and similar functions, most probably you will choose the more aesthetically pleasing option because a common trait of humans is to perceive beautifully designed things as being better. This is the power of a good graphic design.

Have you noticed that all designs generally can be divided in those that look well-designed and in those that don't? Do you know why? Because the creators of those designs that look well-designed have used some basic principles that every professional designer knows, but others – haven't. These principles are applied to all professionally designed advertisements, banners, posters, brochures and other illustrative visuals. The acronym of them is **CRAP: contrast, repetition, alignment, and proximity.** They complement each other; therefore, usually you will use several of them simultaneously. What's important to know is that if you understand these 4 principles, then over time you'll develop a feel for why some designs look good and some - don't. It's like you'll have some secret super-sense.

Contrast

Let's start with the principle of Contrast, which is one of the most powerful design concepts, because it attracts attention, creates hierarchy and helps the viewer to "get" the point of your design quickly. In simple words – contrast is used to emphasize information that is important and to attract viewer eye to start communication. This is why the most important element of your design should be the most emphasized. The second most important element should be less emphasized, and so on. This is how you can create the hierarchy and flow of your design to communicate your marketing message.

Since contrast helps to organize information, users know where to look first, second, third and last. This helps with scanning the visual or a web page. In order to create a successful hierarchy of your design elements that serves their purpose, you need to decide first which phrases and words are the most important and then emphasize them to create the visual hierarchy by making the main message bigger, bolder brighter and so on. For example, the main message of the banner below is the „big sale", which has been emphasized the most.

Contrast does more than just attracts attention. It can be used to establish boundaries between elements, too. For example, if you contrast the background color of the main web page content and that of a sidebar, you show where one ends and the other begins.

Similarly, it can work in advertisement, when you, for example, put the main marketing message on a significantly different background than all the other information.

You can achieve contrast in many ways:

- manipulate the space (empty vs. filled)

- by usage and placement of elements (isolated or grouped and bottom or top)

- through color choices (dark versus light)

- cool colors vs. warm colors

- by size (small vs. big)

- by creating elements that are visually different from the other elements used in your design.

- by using typographic contrasts that I will explain you in one of the next chapters.

Keep in mind that contrast only works well if the difference between elements is APPARENT. If the difference is too small, it may appear to be more of a mistake than a deliberate decision. Create a big difference, in order to differentiate two items from each other. You can't contrast 12px type with 11px type. You see, it looks like a mistake here. You can't contrast black with dark brown either. But if you lower the contrast, you can make an element fade into the background. Therefore, you can use contrast to 'hide' certain elements of your designs as well as to give a special meaning to them.

Risks

Too much contrast can disturb the harmony and unity in a design, leading to chaos and visual noise that causes confusion. Nothing will stand out if every element contrasts and tries to draw attention to itself. Therefore, unless it's your intention, don't overdo the contrast. Instead decide which few elements need to stand out and make them look very different from everything else. Use contrast in moderation.

Repetition

In simple words, the principle of repetition means that you repeat the same or similar design elements throughout the design of your visual. The purpose of this principle is to tie together separate elements of your design and give a sense of unity and consistency. While contrast is used to show differences, the principle of repetition is used to make sure that the design is viewed as a whole. The repetitive elements of the design may be colors, shapes, textures, spatial relationships, line thicknesses, types, sizes, graphic concepts, etc.

Look at the example of these cocktail cards. Although different background colors have been used, both pages still look like taken from one design project and are cohesive, because all other elements – drawing style, typefaces, background pattern and text placement repeat themselves.

In the next example, although both cocktails in the cards are drawn by the same artist and in the same style, the whole image differs and it's apparent that they come from two different projects. If these two pages were put in the same brochure, it would look like that one page is coming from another project and has been put there by a mistake.

As you can see, repetition is especially important when it comes to multi-page design projects, like a brochure, a menu, a book or presentation slides. Therefore, repeating the same design elements, formatting, colors and style will create a cohesive set of pages and consistent design.

However, repetition is also very important in a single page design project. For example, if you have given visually similar characteristics to several elements, then you communicate that something is similar to these elements. If two elements on a visual are both put in black rectangular, a viewer most likely will subconsciously conclude that they are somehow related. For example, look at this banner that I use on my web page. Typefaces, style, and colors are repeated in order to create a united feeling and design, but contrast is used to create accents and draw attention to the main marketing message, which is "Subscribe" to get free course.

Create Your Website Visuals

with FREE TOOLS!

7 days = 7 emails

Subscribe!

Repetition is a key factor in branding and marketing. In order to create your unique brand design, you need to decide what style, two to four colors, types, symbols you will use for all your visual communication. This consistency will help your audience to recognize your brand and company and will evoke certain feelings and emotions associated with your brand. In order to stay consistent with your colors, find and save your brand colors using their codes (HEX, RGB, CMYK). They appear in whatever graphic design software or tool you use when a color is selected on the color palette.

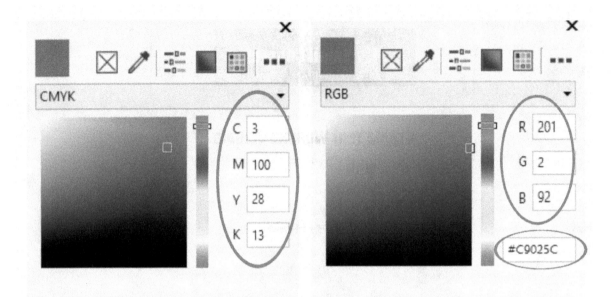

In the example above you see three codes (RGB, CMYK, and HEX) of the same color. In the case, your graphic software or online tool shows only one of them, for example, HEX code, but you need to know also RGB and CMYK codes of the same color, use one of the color code convertors that are available on the Internet, for example, Rapidtables or Hex Colors.

All your images and advertisements both: online and offline must represent your branding with certain colors, fonts, backgrounds, icons, image style and tonality. When you have designed unique visual and textual elements of your brand, repeat those elements through all the visual materials that you create. Through consistency, repetition, and uniqueness of your graphics and materials you will create your brand memorability. As you can see in the example below, all marketing materials that represent your brand, like business cards, letterhead, folder, CD cover and other must have the same style and elements.

Risks

If you aren't consistent with your branding colors, you risk that your logo and colors will be used incorrectly. In the beginning, a little bit different branding color may seem harmless, but in the long term, it can disturb your brand recognition. One more risk is repeating the same element so often that it becomes annoying or overwhelming. For example, if you have chosen a button "Click here" as one of your design elements, don't use it at every link you have on your web page.

Alignment

In this chapter, I'll discuss the principle of alignment. Although on one hand, this concept is very simple and self-evident, on the other hand - if implemented incorrectly, you can get unprofessional results. This is why I feel it should be discussed deeper to help you avoid amateurish mistakes.

The main point of the alignment principle is that nothing in your design should look as if it was placed there randomly because alignment helps unify all of your elements together into a strong and cohesive structure. If you have many elements in your design, imagine that every element and in some cases even details of the element are connected visually with each other via an invisible line – either horizontally, vertically or diagonally. Every element should be aligned to another element (top, bottom, left, right, center to page, vertical center or horizontal center), even if the two objects are physically far away from each other. This creates a clean, sophisticated and professional look. Don't just throw everything on a page like in the example below. No element has been aligned there.

The purpose of the alignment is to organize elements so that their edges or centers are on one line or margin. It doesn't have to be a visible line, most often it is an invisible line implied by the way your design elements are placed.

Edge alignment is used to position elements in a way that their edges are on one line. Either horizontally, vertically or diagonally.

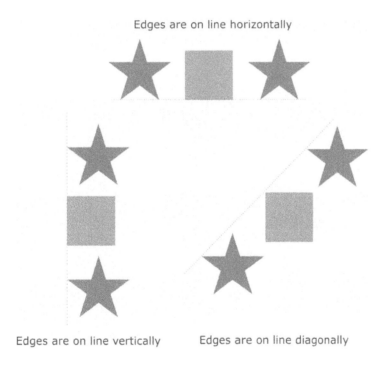

Center alignment is used to line up the design elements with their center axes either horizontally, vertically or diagonally. It doesn't always mean that elements should be placed in the horizontal center of the page. Instead, they can be placed diagonally or side-by-side and still be aligned with their center axes.

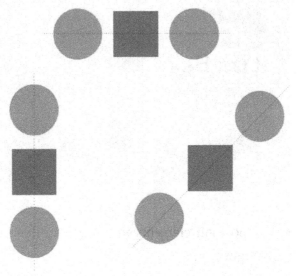
Centers are aligned horizontally

Centers are aligned vertically   Centers are aligned diagonally

4 Ways to Align Your Design Elements

In general, there are four ways you can align elements in your design. Most probably you have already used them every time you type something on your computer as most of us. However, let's discuss them from the perspective of design.

Centered alignment	Right alignment	Left alignment	Justified alignment
Content is placed down the middle	Content is aligned to the right	Content is aligned to the left	Content is placed evenly between two margins

Centered alignment

One of the easiest types of alignment is centered alignment. Centered text works best if used for short lines of text and headlines, because longer texts would be more difficult to read. Usually, centered alignment is a common choice of beginning graphical designers. The problem is, if you use centered alignment without creativity, it might look rather boring and won't create a visual interest.

It is advisable to play with texts, shapes, colors and fonts to attract your audience. As you can see in the example below the word „chef" is emphasized, because this is a job advertisement with a purpose to get noticed by potential chefs, which makes the visual more targeted and visually appealing.

Look at the invitation example below. Actually, all you need is imagination and creativity to create sophisticated and professionally looking centered designs.

You can use centered alignment like this, too. Who said it always has to be horizontal?

Look at this web banner! This centered alignment doesn't look boring thanks to the many colorful elements and contrast.

Be creative when using centered alignment and you will get interesting and eye-catching designs.

Left Alignment

Left Alignment called also Flush Left means that text or graphical elements are lined up evenly with the left margin, but not with the right margin. Left alignment is a good choice if you have large paragraphs of text. If you left align your paragraphs, remember to left align also your headlines.

Centered Headline

Never combine a centered headline with a left aligned paragraph, because readers can have impression that the headline is slightly off-center.

You can safely use left alignment for large paragraphs of text in left to right languages because it doesn't reduce readability. This is one of the most often used ways of alignment.

Left Alignment

Left Alignment called also Flush Left means that text or graphical elements are lined up evenly with the left margin, but not with the right margin. Left alignment is a good choice if you have large paragraphs of text.

Remember!

If you left align your paragraphs, remember to left align also your headlines.

The strong invisible line of the left alignment connects together all texts in this business card.

RB

Robert Brown
Designer

www.brown.com
info@brown.com
455.8652.9102

A good practice is to use explicit lines, too. If you have an image or other elements with explicit outline, align the text along with it as shown in the example below. Therefore, you will create two explicit lines that will be next to each other and create a powerful and interesting effect. In this example, the text is left aligned along the edge of image, which gives it a sophisticated look.

Please join us for a cocktail party!

Friday February 3
6pm until midnight

Cocktail Bar
7 Alderman Ave.
Illinois
600709

RSVP to Jenny
email@email.com

In the next example, you can see how the same design would look if you had ignored the rule of the explicit lines and used a centered alignment instead of the left alignment. As you can see that wouldn't look so sophisticated.

You can add some creativity and use explicit lines in various ways. Who said there always should be only one explicit line?

Right Alignment

Right Alignment called also Flush Right means that text is lined up evenly with the right margin, but not with the left margin. It is often used to give your design a unique and unconventional look. Right alignment works well with short texts, but you should avoid using it on large paragraphs since in the left-to-right languages it decreases readability, but it works well for business cards, for example.

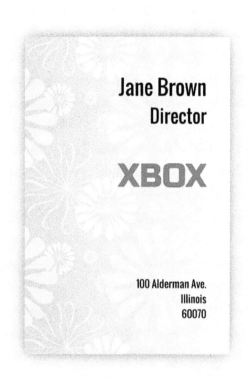

Right alignment often gives more interesting designs than centered alignment but overusing it may annoy your reader. However, if you use it for a design of your letterhead, it might look rather stylish.

Keep in mind that if you need to create your design for right-to-left reading languages (for example, Arabic, Japanese, Korean etc.), then the rules of right alignment substitute the rules of left alignment.

Justified alignment

Justified alignment is created by aligning your text evenly along the left and right margins. This is accomplished by reducing or increasing the spaces between characters and words in each line so that lines with fewer characters will be more broadly spaced, while lines with more characters will have less space between them. This type of alignment, if done correctly, gives more formal and organized look. Most often it is used in books, newspapers, magazines and has become popular on the web, as well. Justified alignment can be especially helpful for working with text in multiple columns because it helps to keep the columns visually separate from each other.

Justified alignment is created by aligning your text evenly along the left and right margins. This is accomplished by reducing or increasing the spaces between characters and words in each line so that lines with fewer characters will be more broadly spaced, while lines with more characters will have less space between them.

Justified alignment is created by aligning your text evenly along the left and right margins. This is accomplished by reducing or increasing the spaces between characters and words in each line so that lines with fewer characters will be more broadly spaced, while lines with more characters will have less space between them.

Basically, alignment makes things easier to read and scan visuals faster. Aligning your elements in a logical way also helps you lead your audience to read your message in the right sequence, which increases the conversion rate.

Risks

If you make your elements almost aligned but not precisely, your design will look less sophisticated. You may think that it is not a big problem, but your audience will unconsciously notice that and perceive the design as less professional, which will damage your brand image.

Another common mistake of new designers is trying to center everything on the page because it's very safe and comfortable. And it makes everything look better. However, actually, it might be a boring and dull approach unless used with creativity as in the examples I showed you. If you don't feel very creative, the much safer choice is aligning your elements to the left or right side. You can also put them on the bottom of the page instead of the centre, for example. Therefore, with careful use of the principles mentioned in this book, your design will definitely look better and more professional. Until you get more practice, it's advisable to use a single strong alignment scheme in one design, because getting several alignment schemes to work in the same design is rather difficult and needs a good expertise and designer sense.

Advanced Text Alignment Techniques

Three more advanced text alignment options that you can use are text wrap, asymmetric and concrete.

Text wrap is used to wrap texts around illustration, photo or another text (for example, large initial letter). This text alignment type is often used in reports, newsletters, books and other text-based designs.

Lorem ipsum dolor sit amet, consectetur adipiscing elit. Nullam ut venenatis massa, egestas auctor est. Nullam dapibus urna a euismod pretium. Maecenas sodales rhoncus nunc in lacinia. nunc eu eros suscipit eget Vestibulum in ultrices lorem leo. Nulla leo consequat eu pulvinar, dapibus convallis lectus. Ut hendrerit lorem pellentesque dolor pellentesque fermentum. Ut pulvinar auctor erat sed congue. Praesent hendrerit vitae sem et hendrerit. Nullam auctor ullamcorper elementum. Quisque sollicitudin arcu eget massa porttitor luctus.

Praesent quis quis suscipit quis lectus. turpis tempus, eget, maximus nulla eu velit, quis dolor velit

Asymmetric text alignment can be used as an interesting design element, for example, in cases when good readability is not the main prerequisite, like, invitations and greeting cards. When asymmetric text alignment is used, few if any, of the text line ends and beginnings align with each other. Therefore, it should not be used for long texts unless there is a good reason for that. This alignment type is creative and informal.

Lorem ipsum dolor sit amet,
consectetur adipiscing elit.
Nullam ut venenatis massa,
egestas auctor est. Nullam
dapibus urna a euismod pretium.
Maecenas sodales rhoncus nunc
in lacinia. Praesent quis nunc eu
eros suscipit suscipit eget quis
lectus. Vestibulum in turpis
t e m p u s ,
ultrices lorem
eget, maximu

consect

Concrete text alignment is used to arrange text to create a concrete shape. For example, it can be used to emphasize the object that is described in the text that creates the shape.

Lore   d e r
m i p s u m   d o l o r s i t
a   m   e   t   ,   c o n s e c t e t u r
adipiscing elit. Nullam ut venenatis
massa, egestas auctor est. Nullam
dapibus urna a euismod pretium.
Maecenas sodales rhoncus
nunc in lacinia. Praesent quis
nunc eu eros suscipit
suscipit eget quis
l e c t u s .
Vestibul
um

Lore
m ipsum dolor sit
amet, consectetur
adipiscing elit. Nullam ut
venenatis massa, egestas
auctor est. **Nullam dapibus urna
a euismod pretium. Maecenas
sodales rhoncus nunc in
lacinia. Praesent quis nunc eu
eros suscipit suscipit eget
quis lectus. Vestibulum
in turpis tempus,**
ultrices lorem

Proximity

Your design always should be easy to scan and perceive. Your audience should never have to make effort at trying to figure out your advertisement organization and design priority, like, which text goes with which graphic or which title comes first and which comes second. The design must be clean and well organized. The main purpose of proximity is to reduce clutter, organize information, and give your reader a clear structure to improve readability. When you are creating your design, be aware of where your eye goes first, second and third when you step back and look at it. Count the number of visual elements on the page and the number of times your eye stops. If your eye stops more than three to five times, consider the grouping of separate items in units to organize the information and reduce clutter.

In order to achieve that, related elements and information should be grouped closely together so that they become one visual unit. When you format a large amount of text in your text editor or any graphical design software, you know which information should be emphasized. To make the formatting more effective and your text easier readable, use the principle of proximity by grouping it. Make bolder and bigger the most important texts like titles and make small the information that is not so important.

In a very simple example, it looks like this.

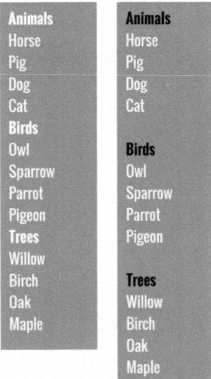

The same principle applies to graphic elements. Here you see a bunch of random squares that really have no proximity to one another. You see each one of these as a separate element; therefore, your eye has to process each of them separately.

Now here are the same squares grouped. Some of them are in more proximity to each other. Although they don't contain any information, you automatically perceive them as three groups.

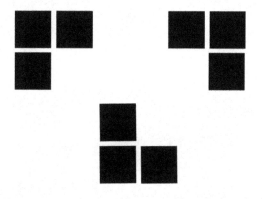

If you want to create no doubt that two elements belong together, make them overlap. That is the strongest proximity relationship.

In the real world, it might look like this. There is no doubt that these three elements have a strong proximity relationship and form a group.

Not like in this example, where all elements are placed randomly.

You can use also other design elements to create proximity relationships. For example, frame your objects or link them with lines or shapes.

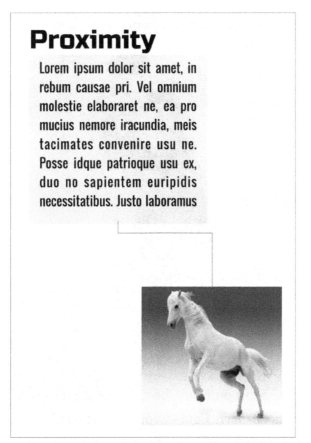

If we use a banner as example, then it is advisable that all related information, like, information about promo offer is placed closely together to form a visual unit. In the example below I have followed this principle; therefore, you have a logical sequence for your eyes to follow.

Don't spread the information over all the area and in each corner like in the example bellow.

Did your eye stop five times? Most probably, because the elements are not logically grouped and there are five elements on this banner. I guess you got confused a little bit because it is difficult to understand the hierarchy of elements. You see, with the help of the principles described in this book you can either direct your reader's eyes and help him/her to understand where to begin and finish reading your message or confuse your reader.

Please see this example of a short article. I have done some basic formatting there. The text is readable but boring. It doesn't arise any visual interest.

3 Tips to Create a Good Logo Design for Your Startup or Blog!

1. Go through these steps, before you start creating your logo:
- Describe your target audience – gender, age, interests, customer income level (high vs. low), decide if your product is a commodity or a premium class product etc.
- Choose your brand name
- Write your slogan or tagline

2. Be creative. When you are thinking about your new logo and business name you should first decide what associations and feelings you want to evoke in your customers. Your logo is not only an image, but it's also an introduction to your brand. When designing your logo, keep in mind that your logo must reach a specific audience.

3. Avoid the clichés. Globes for 'international', handshakes for 'business solutions' and light bulbs for 'ideas' etc. These associations are often the first things that come into your mind when generating ideas; however they should be discarded. How is your logo going to be unique when there are so many other similar logos in your industry?

Find out more: www.digginet.com

Now I have utilized all of the CRAP principles. The same information has been grouped into several groups by adding spacing between the main points. Description of points goes together with the headings, indicating that they are related.

3 Tips to Create a Good Logo Design for Your Startup or Blog!

1. **Go through these steps, before you start creating your logo:**
- Describe your target audience – gender, age, interests, customer income level (high vs. low), decide if your product is a commodity or a premium class product etc.
- Choose your brand name
- Write your slogan or tagline

2. Be creative.
When you are thinking about your new logo and business name you should first decide what associations and feelings you want to evoke in your customers. Your logo is not only an image, but it's also an introduction to your brand. When designing your logo, keep in mind that your logo must reach a specific audience.

3. Avoid the clichés.
Globes for 'international', handshakes for 'business solutions' and light bulbs for 'ideas' etc. These associations are often the first things that come into your mind when generating ideas; however they should be discarded. How is your logo going to be unique when there are so many other similar logos in your industry?

Find out more: www.digginet.com

Notice how by simply changing the typeface, you can change the mood and emotions of the same message. This is how one small change can impact your whole design and the message and emotions it communicates.

> ### 3 Tips to Create a Good Logo Design for Your Startup or Blog!
>
> 1. Go through these steps, before you start creating your logo:
> - Describe your target audience – gender, age, interests, customer income level (high vs. low), decide if your product is a commodity or a premium class product etc.
> - Choose your brand name
> - Write your slogan or tagline
>
> 2. Be creative.
>   When you are thinking about your new logo and business name you should first decide what associations and feelings you want to evoke in your customers. Your logo is not only an image, but it's also an introduction to your brand. When designing your logo, keep in mind that your logo must reach a specific audience.
>
> 3. Avoid the clichés.
>   Globes for 'international', handshakes for 'business solutions' and light bulbs for 'ideas' etc. These associations are often the first things that come into your mind when generating ideas; however they should be discarded. How is your logo going to be unique when there are so many other similar logos in your industry?
>
> Find out more: www.digginet.com

Risks

Very often new designers put text and graphic elements randomly all over the page, filling corners and using a lot of space. It looks like they are afraid to leave some areas empty, which leads to a scattered and unorganized structure and information that is difficult to perceive. If elements are placed randomly, audience unconsciously will assume that they are not closely related. If it is not your intention, don't put elements close to the unrelated group. Otherwise, it can create confusion and you can end up with a clutter. Don't be afraid of empty or actually so-called white space, because it is a very important element of a design. I will tell you how to use white space effectively in a separate chapter later in this book.

What is Composition?

In simple words, composition is when all the separate elements come together to form a whole piece of art and when all your graphic elements, colors, fonts and shapes form one cohesive design. A successful composition means that you have efficiently used and implemented all the CRAP principles discussed in the previous chapter. Therefore, your design not only looks good but is also highly functional and effective.

Visual Balance

All elements in every design should create a visual balance. An important part of this principle is **visual weight,** which is a measure of how much any element in your design attracts the eye of the viewer, for example, large objects appear visually heavier than small objects, but bright colors appear heavier than dark ones. It is a measure of how much something attracts your eye.

If you arrange all the elements so that no one part is overpowering, visual balance is achieved. If two objects or object groups on both sides of the picture weigh the same, then they are balanced. However perfectly balanced pictures tend to be boring, therefore a certain degree of imbalance can be useful to create visual tension and movement within a composition and make it look more interesting.

4 Types Of Composition Balance

The composition may be balanced or unbalanced. The balanced composition feels stable and aesthetically pleasing. While some of its elements might attract your eye more than others, no one area of the composition draws your eye so much that you can't see the other areas. On the other hand, in unbalanced composition individual elements dominate the whole design and some information may go unnoticed.

In some situations, unbalanced composition might be right for the message you're trying to communicate but generally you want balanced compositions.

There are four ways to balance a composition:

1. **Symmetrical balance** is when equal weights are on equal sides of a composition, balanced around a fulcrum or axis in the center. There are two primary types of symmetry:

- **Reflection symmetry** occurs when everything on one side of the axis is mirrored on the other side. It's probably the first thing you think of when you hear the word "symmetry." The axis can be in any direction or orientation, although it's often vertical or horizontal.

A face and a butterfly are common examples of symmetrical balance.

In symmetrical designs, design elements are mirrored from side to side and they often go hand in hand with a centered alignment. The banner below is a good example.

When the reflection is a perfect mirror image, the symmetry is said to be pure. Usually it won't be perfect and each side will have slight variations. This is near symmetry, and it's more common than pure symmetry. The symmetry can even occur over multiple axes at the same time. For example, the left and right half of a composition could mirror each other, while the top and bottom also mirror each other. Snowflakes show reflection symmetry over more than two axes.

- **Rotational symmetry** (or radial symmetry) occurs when everything rotates around a common center. It can occur at any angle or frequency, as long as there's a common center. Natural forms that grow or move perpendicular to the earth's surface develop rotational symmetry. Petals of a flower are a good example. Rotation without reflection can be used to show motion, speed or dynamic action. Think of the spinning wheels of a moving car.

If you're looking to create a strong focal point, rotational symmetry is an effective technique because your eyes are naturally directed to the center.

Symmetry is usually seen as beautiful and harmonized; however, it can also be seen as static and sometimes regarded as boring. Because half of the composition mirrors the other half, therefore at least half of the composition will be rather predictable. Asymmetry tends to be more interesting and dynamic.

2. **Asymmetrical balance** results from unequal visual weight on each side of the composition. It is more dynamic and interesting and evokes feelings of modernism, movement, energy and vitality. Asymmetry creates more complex relationships between elements, and so it tends to be more interesting than symmetry. Because it's more interesting, asymmetry helps to draw attention.

One of the easiest ways to create an asymmetrical balance is to draw an invisible line down the middle of your layout and arrange your design elements unequally on either side of the line.

In general, there are several principles of asymmetrical balance you should know:
- Large elements seem heavier and attract more attention than small ones

- Dark elements feel heavier and draw more attention than light ones

- Objects with texture draw more attention than objects without texture

- One visually heavy element might be balanced out by many lighter elements

- One element on a page is more eye-catching than one of many

- Bright and warm colors are more eye-catching than neutral or cool colors

Asymmetry is rather common in natural forms: you're probably right- or left-handed; trees branches grow in different directions; clouds have random shapes.

Overall you have more freedom of expression with asymmetry than with symmetry. Much in the same way that similarity and contrast work together, you can combine symmetry and asymmetry to good effect. Balance symmetrical forms in an asymmetrical way, or balance asymmetrical forms symmetrically. Contrast symmetry and asymmetry in your composition to make elements get more attention.

In the example below you can see that otherwise very symmetrical composition has been improved with a horse and asymmetrical shape of the rectangular, which are the only elements there that don't repeat themselves. If you took them away, the design would look rather boring.

3. Mosaic or crystallographic balance can be compared with a balanced chaos. This type of balance lack distinct focal points and hierarchy and has many repeating elements that have the same visual weight. Thanks to the sophisticatedly repeated shapes, colors, and sizes a feel of visual balance is created. Please see two examples of crystallographic balance in the images below.

When you're designing, try experimenting with different kinds of compositional balance and CRAP principles. See what works best for your design, project, and brand. Elements of your composition can be arranged in such a way that they have one kind of balance or another. To better understand the compositional principles, educate your eyes and study your favorite examples of graphic design. Try to recognize how different elements in the composition are being used to counterbalance others and determine, when composition is balanced and when it is not. You can even try to recognize which type of compositional balance is being used in every case.

Visual Direction and Flow

Visual direction is the direction in which we unconsciously think an element would be moving if it were given a chance to move in the page. It is often used to lead the viewer's eye to the specific information or element.

You can lead your viewer's eye with the help of an illustration or a photography, too. A common rule is that if an image of a person is used, make sure the person is looking to the main message of your design. See the simple example below.

Cat Food Sale!

American designer Charles Eames have said: „Design is a plan for arranging elements in such a way as best to accomplish a particular purpose." With the help of flow, you can create a visual and verbal sequence in which your viewer will read and scan your design and marketing message. In order to create an effective flow, you must purposefully arrange all the visual elements in a way that controls and leads your viewer's eye to the direction you want. It's advisable to use the principle of flow in every design you create. For example, in the example below, this principle is successfully used to lead your potential client eyes from the word „sale" to „up to 30% off", which is the main message of this banner. It was done with the simple black triangle that connects both messages together.

Optical Center

Everybody knows what geometrical center is. If we draw two diagonal lines through the plane (whether it's picture, a piece of paper or a computer monitor), the intersection point shows the geometric center of the composition.

Optical center is the spot that attracts the viewer's eye the most unless other visual elements draw it elsewhere. Usually **vertical optical center** sits slightly above the geometric center. In advertising, the selection of the optical center may be useful to draw the attention of the potential buyer to the specific information. This may be marketing message or an image.

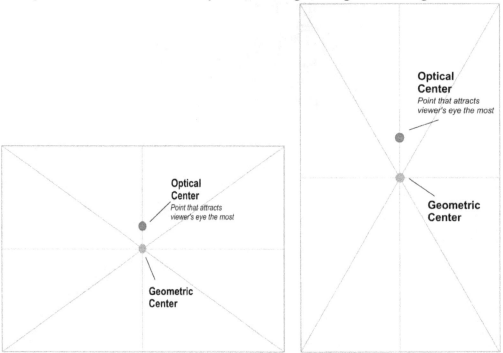

Optical center can be emphasized with:
- contrast
- size
- form
- design elements

It doesn't mean that you always must put all your most important information in the vertical optical center, but you should keep in mind that this is how the human eye works. It's a good rule of thumb to make wider margin in the bottom of your page or whatever design project you create and narrower margin in the top of the page. Therefore, you will naturally place all your information slightly closer to the optical center. Because if you leave both margins in the same size it may look like your elements are dropping out of the page a bit. Look at the example below. The picture here is perfectly centered and distance of both margins – upper and bottom are exactly the same size. However, because of the vertical optical center. it looks like the picture is placed slightly too low.

On the other hand, in the next example, the picture has been placed considering the vertical optical center and the bottom margin is left a little bit wider than the top margin. Therefore, the picture looks placed perfectly in the right place.

Additionally, it is important to consider the **horizontal optical center** (of both the object and space) when you want to achieve a centered alignment for an object that has an irregular form. The object in the example below has been perfectly centered in the middle of the rectangular. If you measured with a ruler, the margins on each side of the page would be exactly the same. However, because of the optical illusion, it looks like it has been placed slightly more to the left side.

In order to make this object look like it has been placed perfectly in the center of the page, it must be moved manually a little bit more to the right. Actually, the margins will not be in the same size anymore, but when viewed, the object appears balanced.

White Space

Each design starts with a white space. In the beginning, it's undefined white space, which is what you get when you take a clean page or open a new document. When you put elements in the undefined white space, active white space occurs, which is an important part of every design. White space or also called negative space is always a necessary element in any good design. Don't misinterpret, white space is just a term. Actually, **it can be any color** – red, yellow, black or whatever color or background texture you use in your design. In the example below the white space is actually red. Its main purpose is to reduce noise and clutter so that focal elements of the design can be easily recognized and perceived.

How to Create White Space in Your Design?

1. Don't be afraid of empty space in your design and don't fill up your layout with text and graphic elements. The empty space is actually functioning as the white space, and you need it for creating a good-looking design.

2. If you feel like you need to create more white space to increase contrast around your focal points, consider scaling down all of your design elements (graphic and type) or just few of them.

3. Ask yourself if you really need all these titles, texts, and images in your design? By deleting the unnecessary elements, you can create a more focused and professional design. If you are not sure about the necessity of an element, most probably you don't

need it and it can be deleted.

4. Think outside of the box and look, if you can create some hidden elements like in the examples below that will give your design a really sophisticated look.

With the help of the white space, you can mold and define what the positive space is. See a classical example of optical illusion below. This is how you can create hidden elements and give additional meaning to the content. Like in this example, by creating two elements you actually get three elements. What do you see? Two faces or a vase?

And what do you see in the next example – a flower or two dragons?

This strategy works great when creating a logo, too. Using white space creatively you can incorporate multiple meanings in your logo design. Here are some examples of big organization logos where white space has been used effectively. For example, in FedEx logo, the white space between letters "E" and "X" looks like an arrow, which symbolizes speed and moving forward.

The white space works perfectly for the panda logo of World Wildlife Fund and Pitsburgh Zoo, too.

If you want to understand the psychology of shapes, meaning of colors in branding and importance of responsive logo design, you can learn about it in my book "Effective Logo Design: Guidelines for Small Business Owners, Bloggers, and Marketers".

Color as Design Element

Now we have come to the most colorful chapter of this book. Colors can energize or cool down. They can lead to action and increase your conversation rates online of offline if you learn to use them effectively or they can scare away your potential customers if used incorrectly. Colors are one of the most powerful design elements. They attract attention, create associations, and set a mood. Actually, you don't need to invent a bicycle because it is already proven which colors work well together and all professional graphic designers use this knowledge for creating their good-looking designs. You just need to follow the best practices. Let's start with analyzing color wheel and learning the basic terms of color theory and then we will move to a more interesting part of creating color schemes.

Primary, Secondary and Tertiary Colors

As you probably know, you can create any color by mixing the three primary colors: red, yellow, and blue, which are the only colors you can't create by mixing other colors.

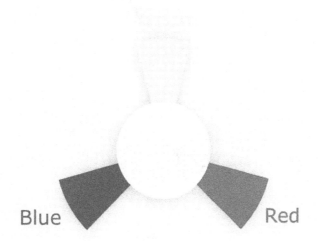

If you mix two primary neighbor colors in equal amounts, you get a secondary color. For example, by mixing yellow and blue, you get green.

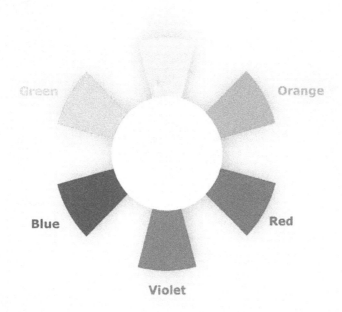

If you move forward and mix each of the adjacent colors, you will get tertiary colors that will fill the empty spaces left in your color wheel.

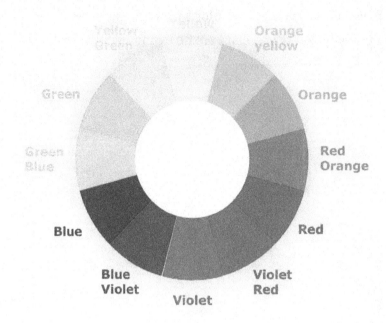

Hues, Tints, Shades and Tones

The six primary and secondary colors that you saw in the previous color wheels are called hues. These are pure colors that are basis for every other color variation. When you add white, black or both to your hues, you can get tints, tones, and shades.

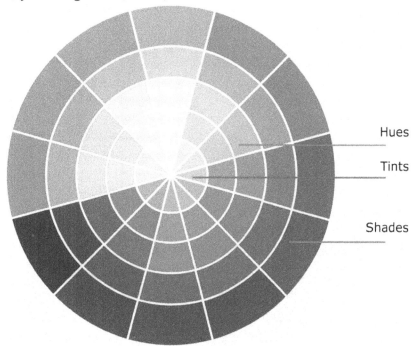

Hues

Tints

Shades

Tints or Pastels

Let's start with lightening the twelve basic hues to create Tints or sometimes called **Pastels**. Basically, tints are simply any color with white added, which lightens and desaturates the hue, making it less intense. Tints are calmer, quieter colors. That means you can go from an extremely pale, nearly white to a barely tinted almost pure hue.

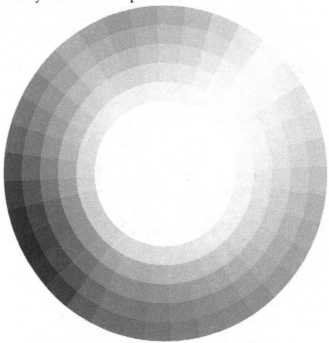

A color scheme using Tints is usually soft, youthful and soothing, especially the lighter versions. All tints work well in feminine environments. You often see advertising, marketing and websites use pale and hot pastels if they are targeting women as a demographic.

Shades

So now that you know how to lighten, what's the easiest way to make your colors darker? A Shade is simply any color with black added. Just as with making tints, you can mix any of the twelve pure colors together. Then simply add any amount of black and you have created a shade of the mixture.

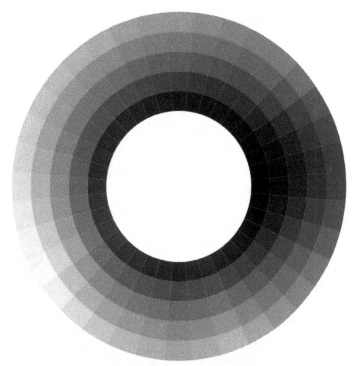

That means you can go from an extremely dark, nearly black to a barely shaded pure hue. Be careful not to use too much black as it can get a little overpowering. These darks work well in a masculine environment and are best used as dark accents in art and marketing graphics.

Tones

Now that you know how to lighten and darken your twelve colors how do you tone them down? Almost every color we see in our day-to-day world has been toned either a little or a lot. This makes for more appealing color combinations. A Tone is created by adding both White and Black which is grey. Any color that is "greyed down" is considered a Tone. Tones are somehow more pleasing to the eye. They are more complex, subtle and sophisticated.

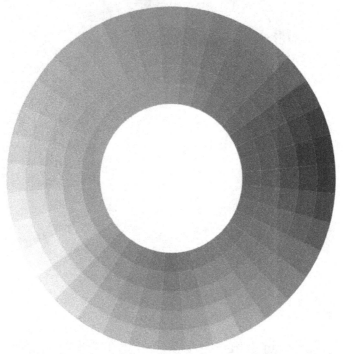

Artists usually mix a little grey in every paint mixture to adjust the value and intensity of their pigment. Tones are the best choice for most interior decorating because they're more interesting. They work well in any Color Scheme you might plan.

Designers are always throwing around terms like warm colors and cool colors. But what do they really mean? Gaining an understanding of these terms will help you determine what to look for when choosing colors for your brand, advertisement or whatever design.

Warm vs. Cool Colors and Hybrids

The color palette is roughly divided into two groups: warm colors on the one side of the color wheel and cool colors on the other side and they are rather self-explanatory. Reds, oranges, yellows, and beige or creamy colors are WARM and they tend to make you think of sunlight and heat. They are hot, stimulating and soothing to our EMOTIONS. But blues, greens, and grays are COOL and they tend to make you think of cold, water and winter. This is rather simple.

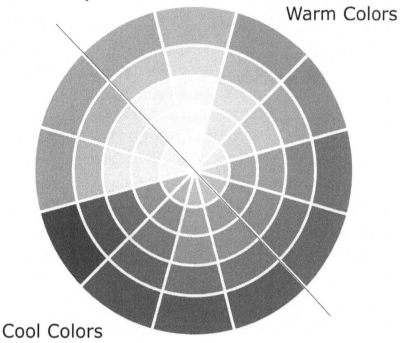

However, there are also color hybrids. These are the colors that are formed when cool and warm colors meet. Hybrids can be warmer or cooler depending on their mix. For example, green and Purple are the hybrids. If green has a lot of yellow in it and forms a lime color, then it is warm, but if it has more blue, then it is cool color (think of Kelly green). But if you add blue to purple color, then you get cool blue-violet color, but if you add red, then you get red violet, which is warm color.

Make Your Own Shades, Tints and Tones

In most graphic design software and online tools, you can create your own colors. If you want to make a shade, just add black. If you need a tint, move the slider closer to the white color. In order to create a tone, add grey.

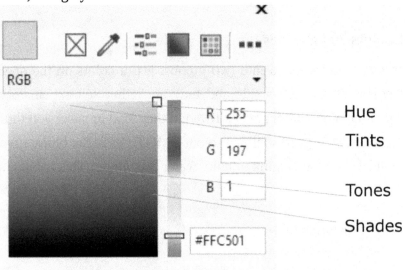

In the next chapter, I'll tell you, how to create different color schemes (complementary, triads analogous or other) by using different principles. Be creative and have fun by combining different shades, pastels, tints and hues and creating your own color schemes according to the basic rules of color relationships you will learn. Instead of using pure hues, select one hue, one shade, and one tint, for example.

Create Your Own Professionally Looking Color Schemes

Now I'll describe the main principles of good looking color schemes. Below each scheme you will find a banner that is designed using the color combination of the scheme described. Therefore, you will be able to see, how easy is to change the mood and associations of the same banner just by using different color combinations.

Complementary Colors

The colors that are positioned opposite one another in the color wheel are complementary colors. In spite of the congenial-sounding name given to these pairs of hues, they come from directly opposing spokes of the color wheel and have absolutely nothing in common. The term opposite colors would actually be more appropriate for describing them.

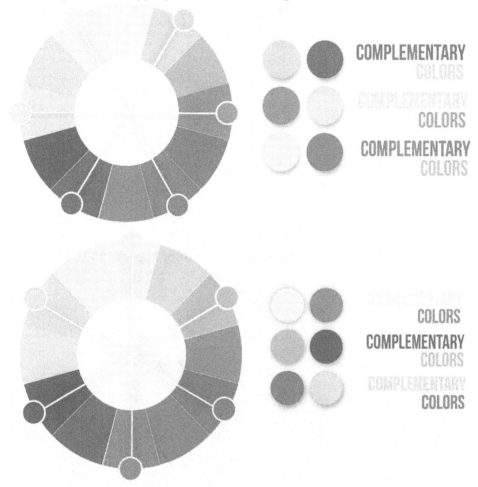

The color wheel is organized so that if opposite colors are chosen, then one color is always cool and the other always warm with the greatest contrast. When complementary colors are placed next to each other, they make the other color look more intense and brighter. They work well when you want to create a contrast or emphasize something in your design. If you place a tiny accent of a color's complement next to it, you will create an emphasis. Look at this bright and colorful web banner created in the complementary color scheme.

However, be careful with the complementary colors to avoid an effect known as *simultaneous contrast, which results in* each color making the other color appear more vibrant and dominant. This can be horribly painful for the viewer's eye.

Double Complementary Colors

Double complementary color scheme is called tetradic because it uses four colors arranged into two complementary color pairs from either side of complementary colors on the color wheel. If you use all four colors in equal amounts, it will be difficult to harmonize them, and the overall impression may look unbalanced. Therefore, it is advisable to use one dominant color in your color scheme. Additionally, avoid using pure colors in equal amounts. This is one of the most complex color schemes that provides a lot of contrast in color while still blending harmoniously if used correctly. Double complementary colors make an X in the color wheel.

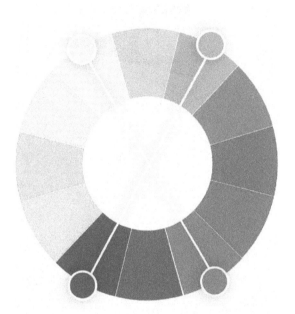

See the example below of this color scheme. There are exactly four colors in this design additionally to black and white. The complements orange and blue have been paired with violet and blue.

Triads

A ***triadic*** color scheme is a set of three different colors on a color wheel that are in equal distance from each other. Red, yellow, and blue are a triadic set of hues. Violet, orange, and green also form a triad, as do blue-violet, red-orange, and yellow-green and so on.

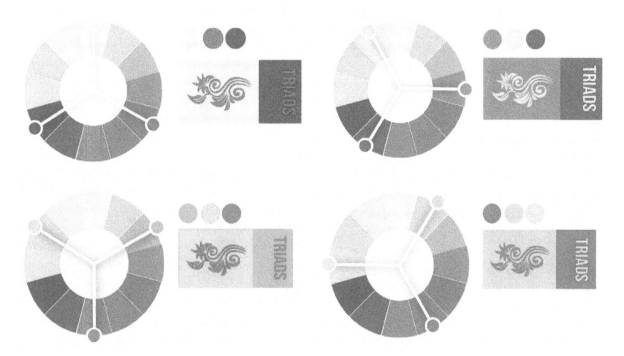

No three hues of the color wheel can be spaced more widely—and therefore be more visually diverse—than those belonging to a triadic palette. This is why color triads are often used in color schemes to create both contrast and balance.

JUST NOW !

FINAL SALE

- 60%

GO SHOPPING >

Split Complementary Colors

A Split Complementary Color Scheme consists of three hues. This palette is created by choosing a base color on the one side of the color wheel and then using the two **colors** adjacent to its **complement**, for example, yellow, joined by red-violet and blue-violet. This provides high contrast that doesn't create tension like the complementary scheme. If you are a beginner, this color scheme can be a good choice to start, because it is difficult to screw up.

Analogous Colors

Combinations of three to five adjacent hues on the color wheel form analogous sets. All of the colors of this set are neighbors and near-neighbors on the color wheel. This is why you should use enough contrast when using an analogous color scheme.

A good rule of thumb is to use one color to dominate and a second to support it, but the third color - as an accent (along with black, grey or white).

Monochromatic Color Scheme

Create a **Monochromatic Color Scheme** by taking any of the Hues and repeating it in various Tints, Shades and Tones. All grayscale images are created in monochromatic color scheme. But you can do it in colors, too. For example, choose Green as a basis for your design project and then use it in tints, shades, and tones, creating as many variations, both obvious and subtle, as you need for your project. It is very sophisticated approach and usually creates a calming effect.

In Conclusion

Each hue of the color-wheel-based color schemes can be darkened, lightened, muted, or brightened. Play with levels of saturation within every color scheme described – soften or increase their brightness (make tints, shades or tones) to get the result you want. There are nearly unlimited color scheme combinations available. Create your own color triads and experiment with the colors schemes *you* can create.

However, to avoid chaos and oversaturation, make one of your colors dominant in your palette. When you understand and gain the feel of how these color combinations work together (and which ones you prefer for yourself), you will have much bigger control over your final design. And most probably the design will look much more sophisticated and professional.

And remember that the best color scheme examples can be found in nature.

11 Free Online Tools that Will Help You to Create Your Own Color Schemes

If you still feel like you need some help for choosing right colors for your corporate style, web page, images and ads, then there are many free online tools available that can help you. Use these tools to create beautiful and tasteful color schemes either from your chosen image or following suggestions of these tools. You can even use already finished color schemes that are created by professional designers. If you know the basics of color theory, you can always create beautiful designs and color combinations. All you need to do is to write down the HEX and RGB codes of the colors you chose to use them for your own graphic design projects. Have fun!

1. Color Calculator: - a free and convenient tool that helps you literary calculate your color schemes. Great tool for creating color schemes using the principles I described before.
2. Coolors – get suggestions for beautiful color schemes with a click of a spacebar.
3. Color Adobe - create color schemes from your image or browse thousands of color combinations. This tool lets you create and save various color schemes, each of which consists of a set of five colors.
4. Color Sphere - Google Chrome plugin that helps you to build up a color scheme from one chosen shade. If you're unsure what color scheme you should choose, Color Sphere provides a selection of themes from a drop-down menu. It helps you harmonize colors, find HEX codes and simulate color-blindness.
5. TinEye Color Extraction - a great tool for creating a color scheme based on your chosen image. You will get a color palette for all the colors identified in your image, including color codes.
6. Get inspiration from color palettes created by professional designers. Just find the color scheme you like in the website Colour Lovers, copy the codes (hex and RGB) and use it for your designs.
7. ColorZilla - a tool that helps you to get color codes from any point in your Internet browser and use it in your design projects. Open any web page, analyze it and inspect a palette of its colors.
8. TinEye Multicolr - if you need to get free images in a specific color combination, search 20 million Creative Commons images from Flickr by color.
9. Color Blindness - this tool will help you to assign a certain color to a main hue. It comprises 1640 different color names. Try it out.
10.   Rapid Tables and Hex Colorrrs - tools for converting color codes from HEX to

RGB or CMYK and vice versa.

How to Choose The Right Colors for Your Project

Each color arises particular emotions and associations. Therefore, when you are choosing colors scheme for your design, consider characteristics of your target audience (age, sex, social group etc.), because what works well for one social group won't work for another. For example, pink color may work great for young girls but won't work at all for a law company.

When creating your brand guidelines or any smaller design project, keep in mind the psychological explanations of colors as described in the infographic below; however, don't forget that different color variations and combinations give different associations and feelings, so be creative and don't follow these general rules blindly. Instead, try to find out what colors and their combinations work best for your brand and be creative.

Color Meaning
in Western Cultures

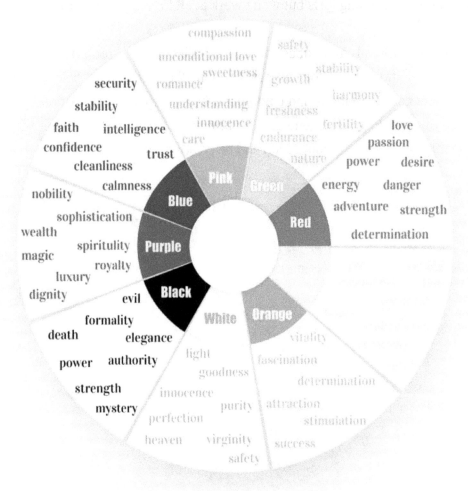

CMYK vs RGB

There are two color models that are commonly used in print and digital design: RGB and CMYK.

What is RGB color used for?

In RGB color model red, green and blue lights are mixed together in different ways to create any color you may need. This color model usually is used for creating and displaying images in electronic systems, such as TVs, computers, and smartphones. Basically, it means that if you are going to create a banner or image that will be used only digitally, choose RGB color model.

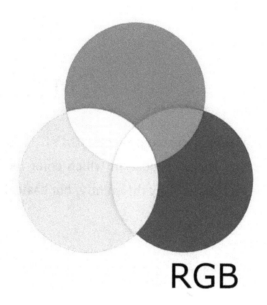

What is CMYK color used for?

CMYK is an abbreviation of cyan, magenta, yellow, and key (black) ink colors that are used for color printing. The four inks are applied one after the other on white paper to produce a full-color image. Therefore, to be sure that your printed colors will match the colors you see on your computer screen, use CMYK color model.

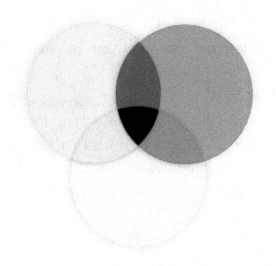

CMYK

So, to put it simply- RGB is for digital design projects, CMYK is for print. If you use advanced graphic design software, you can usually choose in which color mode you want to create your design. Each software provides this possibility differently, but basically, it looks like this.

Create a New Document   ✕

Name:	Untitled-1
Preset destination:	CorelDRAW default ▾
Size:	A4 ▾
Width:	210,0 mm ↕ millimeters ▾
Height:	297,0 mm ↕ ▢ ▭
Number of pages:	1 ↕
Primary color mode:	CMYK ▾
	RGB
Rendering resolution:	CMYK dpi
Preview mode:	Enhanced ▾

▾ **Color settings**

▴ **Description**

Choose a primary color mode for your document. The default color mode affects how colors are blended together in effects such as fills, blends, and transparencies.

☐ Do not show this dialog again

OK   Cancel   Help

Different color combinations work well for different purposes. However not every color combination is good for advertising. Actually, the most important thing in every advertisement is a good readability. If your advertisement message is too difficult to read and perceive, nobody will do that. If nobody reads it, it goes unnoticed. If it goes unnoticed, you don't have any results. No customers, no sales, no money. Just waste of your advertising money. Keep in mind that nowadays due to the lack of time and abundance of the information most often people scan texts instead of reading. Therefore, in order to catch their attention, you need to create easily readable designs and texts.

I have listed few of the color combinations you should avoid when creating your advertisements.

1. **Green and Yellow**

Since yellow and green are too close together, they are difficult to read. There is a lack of contrast that arises interest. Your ad will simply go unnoticed.

2. **Green and Purple**

Although it is possible to make interesting and eye-catching designs from green and purple colors, purple text on a green background may be just too difficult to read. Mix it up with, white, gray and black or use tints and shades to reduce brightness.

3. Light Colors on a White Background

Yes, they look nice and calming but are too difficult to read. Unless you want to hide some information from your advertisement readers, don't use a combination of light colored text on a light background.

4. Neon Colors

Although they look eye-catching, they will tire and irritate your reader's eyes.

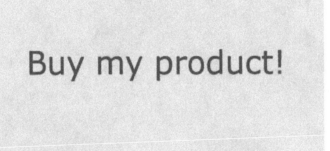

5. Colored and Textured Cackground

Don't put text on a bright colored and textured background or it will be unreadable. Turn down the opacity or place your text in a separate box with a light background to make sure it's readable.

6. Blue and Red

There are many situations when blue and red colors work great together, but not for the texts. Both colors are so strong that they clash terribly.

7. **Dark Backgrounds**

Unless you have a good reason, avoid putting red, blue or purple text on a black background, because they are very hard to read.

Moreover, try to avoid putting white text on a black background, too. As I mentioned before, readers either read or scan texts. If they scan, they notice only most emphasized words. In the case these words rise interest, they start reading to understand the subject. Before you decide to use white text on a dark background consider, if your readers will scan or read the text. Usually, people read paragraph text, but scan headings, titles, and labels. Therefore, while it may be a good choice to use white text on a dark background for titles and headings to highlight them and grab readers attention, it's advisable to not use white text on a dark background for paragraph texts, because that strains the reader's eyes.

HEADLINE!

Your paragraph text. Your paragraph text. Your paragraph text. Your paragraph text.

If you still want to put white paragraph text on a black background, then rather use light gray color, since that will be easier for your reader's eyes.

It's advisable to not use white text on a dark background for paragraph texts, because that strains the reader's eyes.

If you really want to put light text on a black background, then rather use light gray color, since that will be easier for your reader's eyes.

However, there are few situations when advertisers deliberately put a white text on a dark background. For example, if they put some legal information in their advertisement that they want to go unnoticed. Leasing interest rates, for example, or additional costs. In this case, some marketers deliberately put white text on a black background and make the text particularly small to reduce the readability even more.

Fonts or Typefaces?

Most probably you have heard these terms many times, but unless you are a professional designer you have only a vague idea of what the difference between them both is. And does the difference exist at all? Actually, yes, there is a difference. One of the major mistakes, when talking about type, is mixing up fonts with typefaces and using them as synonymous. If all you associate fonts with are texts printed in Microsoft Word, it might not feel like a big deal. However, for those who know the difference, inappropriate usage of both terms may sound like a mistake.

In simple words, the difference between a font and a typeface is the same as the difference between songs and an album. If we compare typography with the music world then typeface is like an album, but fonts are like songs. Because *typeface* is **font family** that make up a design of type, but fonts embody a particular size and weight of the typeface. For example, italicized Arial at 12 points is considered a different font than italicized Arial at 14 points, and bolded Calibri in 18 points is a different font than normal Calibri in 12 points. In both cases Arial and Calibri are typefaces, but the particular size and formatting of it are considered a font.

Perfectly Paired Typefaces

New and amazing typefaces are invented every single day and the number of them keeps growing and growing. There are thousands of different typefaces with new ones being created constantly. It's easy to get distracted and select fonts randomly just by assuming that "they look good together." But are you sure? Actually, there are some basic guidelines that will show you what to look for when trying to find typefaces that complement each other. There are 3 basic principles that you need to know to guide you through this process:

1.**Concord**

If you use only one type family without much variety in size, weight, and style, a design is considered to be concordant. In the example below, I'm using one typeface, Roboto. Within the Roboto typeface family, there are several fonts: Regular, Italic, Bold and Bold Italic.

Concord

Lorem ipsum dolor sit amet, consectetur adipiscing elit. Morbi sollicitudin quam eu odio tempus, sed malesuada dolor sagittis. Pellentesque quis feugiat libero. Phasellus placerat, dolor sed consectetur molestie, lorem magna lobortis orci, sed luctus lorem turpis nec nibh. Quisque nec erat lectus. Pellentesque eu urna dignissim magna tempor posuere non non dolor. Suspendisse potenti. Mauris mattis orci sollicitudin justo pulvinar mollis. Morbi non lorem risus.

Proin a tempor sapien, id condimentum nisl.

(Type used: Roboto)

As you can see, the heading is larger and written in Bold Roboto and the body text is written in Regular Roboto. I have also used Bold Roboto, Bold Italic Roboto and there is some Italic Roboto in brackets. Overall, the design is very simple and neat. Nothing surprising or extraordinary, but a good approach, if you want a clean and formal design.

2. Conflict

If you use two typefaces that are similar, conflict occurs, because although the difference is subtle, it is noticeable, and your reader may wonder if it is a mistake. It might sound like it's not a big problem, but it unconsciously disturbs the reader and gives the impression of unprofessionalism. Therefore, make sure that the typefaces you are using are different enough from each other to avoid conflict.

Look at the example below. This time I've put the heading in Gill Sans. Both Gill Sans and Verdana are sans-serif fonts and while they are a little bit different, they still look too similar. If you look at the first and the last sentences in the next example, you will notice that the typeface is different. Even if you haven't noticed that the heading and these sentences are written in a different type, most probably, you have a feeling that it looks like there have been some mistakes in formatting. Remember that when we are dealing with typefaces similarities conflict.

Conflict

Lorem ipsum dolor sit amet, consectetur adipiscing elit. Morbi sollicitudin quam eu odio tempus, sed malesuada dolor sagittis. Pellentesque quis feugiat libero. Phasellus placerat, dolor sed consectetur molestie, lorem magna lobortis orci, sed luctus lorem turpis nec nibh. Quisque nec erat lectus. Pellentesque eu urna dignissim magna tempor posuere non non dolor. Suspendisse potenti. Mauris mattis orci sollicitudin justo pulvinar mollis. Morbi non lorem risus.

Proin a tempor sapien, id condimentum nisl.

(Type used: Verdana, Gill Sans)

3. Contrast

To create a contrast, use typefaces of different and contrasting style. This will help you to create much more attractive and eye-catching designs. The key is to find typefaces that are different but still have enough in common to look good together. It must be apparent that the difference has been created for a reason. You can pair a sans-serif font with a serif font or a fancy font with a classic font. In my example below, I have used Broadway BT type (in titles) combined with Roboto (in body text). This time it's apparent that the heading is written in a different font, which makes the design more attractive and eye-catching.

Contrast

Proin a tempor sapien, id condimentum nisl

Lorem ipsum dolor sit amet, consectetur adipiscing elit. Morbi sollicitudin quam eu odio tempus, sed malesuada dolor sagittis. Pellentesque quis feugiat libero. Phasellus placerat, dolor sed consectetur molestie, lorem magna lobortis orci, sed luctus lorem turpis nec nibh. Quisque nec erat lectus. Pellentesque eu urna dignissim magna tempor posuere non non dolor. Suspendisse potenti. Mauris mattis orci sollicitudin justo pulvinar mollis. Morbi non lorem risus.

(Type used: Roboto, Broadway BT)

To sum it up, concordant typography is good and easy to create, but without a proper formatting, doesn't look very interesting. Don't use conflicting typefaces because this combination doesn't look professional and creates a sense of mistake. If you feel that something is wrong with the combination of your chosen typefaces, make sure they are not too similar and, therefore, conflicting with each other. One of the most interesting choices is using contrasting typefaces because they look attractive and fun. However, remember that the goal of combining several typefaces is to improve the communication, not to confuse your audience.

If you still don't feel sure that you will be able to find the best pair for your chosen font, check out these tools.

Tools for Font Pairing
- http://fontjoy.com/ - generate new font pairings. Replace their text with your book title and tagline. Then choose from different fonts that are suggested for pairings.
- http://www.typeconnection.com – this is like a fun dating game for typefaces. Choose from one of their suggested types and then from four different strategies to find the best match for the chosen typeface. Enjoy the result.
- http://typespiration.com – check out this webpage to find free inspirational font combinations with color palettes made by professional designers.

Or check out Font Bundles where you can download beautiful typefaces that are already paired according to the best practices. There are both free and paid fonts available.

4 Typeface Categories

To understand how typefaces are categorized and what principles are behind their pairing, it is vital to have the basic understanding of the main type groups. They can be broken into 4 very broad categories:

1. Serif or Roman typefaces

A serif is a small line attached to the end of a stroke in a letter or symbol. Therefore, typefaces with serifs are called serif typefaces and most often are used in printed materials: books, newspapers, magazines, and formal documents. They will help your book convey a feeling of traditions, respectability and stability. Serif typefaces are broken into three subcategories, which are commonly used nowadays: Old Style, Transitional, and Modern.

- **Old Style** typefaces were originally created between the late 15th and mid-18th centuries and were mimicking the hand lettering of scribes. They look to be handwritten with a wedge-tipped pen. The main characteristics of this type are a moderate transition between the thick and thin strokes of a letterform, a diagonal stress so that weight stress is at approximately 8:00 and 2:00 o'clock in the thinnest parts of the curved strokes and slanted serifs. This is a good type group to use on a large amount of text because it makes it easy to read.

Type: Goudy Old Style

Few more Old Style type examples:

Radley

Garamond

Palatino

- **Transitional typefaces** were established by English printer and typographer, John Baskerville in the mid-18th century, because of the improved printing methods, which allowed much finer character strokes. Transitional typefaces represent the transition between Old style and the Modern period, and therefore incorporate some characteristics of each. They have a greater contrast between thick and thin strokes and wider, gracefully bracketed serifs with flat bases.

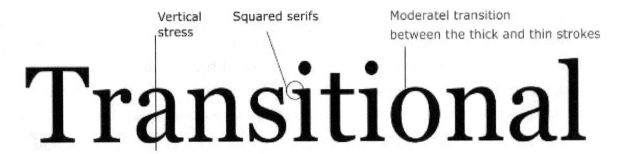

Vertical stress

Squared serifs

Moderatel transition between the thick and thin strokes

Transitional

Type: Georgia

Few more Transitional type examples:

Bookman

Cambria

Century

- **Modern,** also known as Didone typefaces, were developed in the late 18th and early

19th **century,** when even more sophisticated printing techniques and paper were invented. They have thin, horizontal serifs, a radical difference between the thick and thin strokes of a letterform, and a perfectly vertical stress. These typefaces tend to look elegant and really eye-catching, but because of their structure, are also cold. Most of them are less readable than old style typefaces. Modern typefaces work well as headlines but are not good for body text, either on the web or in print. Because of their prominent thick lines, the thin lines almost disappear when used for body copy in print, and therefore an effect called "dazzling" occurs, which significantly reduces readability.

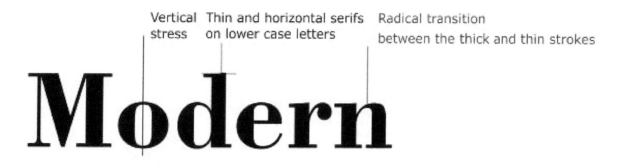

Type: Bodoni Bd BT

Few more Modern type examples:

Onyx

PLAYFAIR DISPLAY SC
Modern No. 20

2. Sans serif typefaces

The Sans serif term comes from the word "sans," which in French means "without," because these typefaces do not have the small serifs at the end of their strokes. Simply speaking, these are typefaces without serifs. They often have minimal variation in stroke width, creating the impression of a minimal, simplified design. Most sans serifs are mono-weight, but very few of them have a slight thick to thin transition. They are contemporary and rather universal. Often, they are used for body text, on-screen online as well as for book headlines and printed materials. The well-known Arial, popularized by Microsoft, is a common Sans serif example.

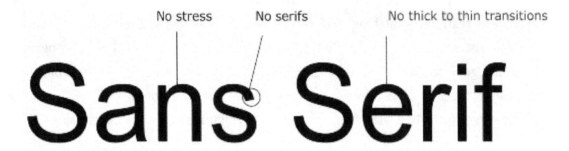

Type: Arial

Few more Sans Serif type examples:

Segoe UI
DejaVu Sans
Roboto

3. Script typefaces

These typefaces imitate handwriting. This category can be broken down into scripts that connect and scripts that don't, calligraphic scripts, scripts that look like they're hand printed, and so on. Be careful when using scripts – don't overdo them and never use them in all caps, because that would look annoying and disturb readability. Usually, they aren't used for body text because they are harder to read than many serif and sans-serif typefaces. However, they can be successfully used as an interesting accent and fancy design element. In general, scripts are used for logos, invitations, displays, and headlines. They inspire feelings of elegance, grace and femininity and make the texts look more personal.

Script

Type: Lucida Handwriting

Few more Script type examples:

Bradley Hand ITC

Kaufmann BT

Palace Script MT

4. Decorative Typefaces

Decorative typefaces became popular in the 19th century and were used extensively on posters and advertisements. They are good for conveying specific emotions and are funny, artistic, and attractive. Decorative typefaces work great for eye-catching headlines but are not appropriate for body text, because that would be annoying and unreadable. It's advisable to use them in a limited amount.

Type: HotSweat

Few more Decorative type examples:

AMAZDOOM

KOMIKA GLAZE

GUN METAL

Typographic Contrasts

According to Canadian typographer Carl Dair, there are 7 different ways how you can contrast types.

1. **Size**

It's the most basic and simple way to use contrast. Just use a small type with a big type. Usually, this way of contrast is used by making headlines much bigger than the body text.

simple way to use
contrast

2. **Weight**

Use bold type versus light type of the same style to emphasize some part of the text or create an interesting effect.

bold type versus light type

3. **Form**

Basically, contrast by form is used every time you use a capital letter together with a lower case. Actually, you are using this contrast every time you write a sentence. You can contrast by form also when use condensed typefaces together with expanded typefaces.

CONTRAST of form

4. **Structure**

Various typefaces have different letterform and structure. The best way to contrast them is by using two typefaces from two different categories of type. For example, you can contrast a san serif type with a modern typeface or a script. It's advisable to not use two different typefaces from one category on the same page to avoid conflict.

CONTRAST **of structure**

5. Texture

You can create an effect of texture by using lines with text in large blocks. Therefore, the text is perceived as a whole. Experiment with different typefaces and letterforms to get the most interesting result.

texture
texture
contrast **of texture**
texture
texture

6. Color

Like you already read in the very first chapter about contrast, you can surely create contrast with colors, too, for example, cool vs. warm, light vs. dark, using complementary colors and so on. Just use the same principles you have already learned in the previous chapter about creating good looking color schemes. And don't forget that black-and-white creates the most powerful contrasts.

contrast of color

7. Direction

Every element of a type and letter has a direction. A line with a text has a horizontal direction, but a narrow column with a text has a vertical direction. If you contrast them both, you can get a really sophisticated design. You can also mix wide blocks of long lines with tall columns of short lines to create an interesting design.

CONTRAST OF DIRECTION

Lorem ipsum dolor sit amet, mel no ferri tantas, vis sonet accumsan ex, no liber torquatos democritum vim. Has aperiam aliquam ne, ea pri vero malis habemus. Eam latine netrik intellegam accommodare ne, cum delenit pertinax evertitur ut, ne cum dolores assueverit. Quo te convenire molestiae, persius commune his eu, has invenire inimicus no. Cu nam facilis consequat, ei est eius prima aperiam. Regione dolores necessitatibus vis ex, vix suas nostrud eu. Lorem ipsum dolor sit amet, mel no ferri tantas, vis sonet accumsan ex, no liber torquatos democritum vim. Has aperiam aliquam ne, ea pri vero malis habemus. Eam

One more way how to use the contrast by direction is to put your text diagonally. If you want to create a positive and forward energy, place it with angle up to the right, if you want to create a downward energy, then with an angle down to the right. Experiment with using both angles on one page to create eye-catching designs. Just don't neglect the readability while doing that.

Usually, we use several types of contrast together. Most often even without recognizing that. Hopefully, now, when you have learned about these typographic contrast principles, you will use them consciously and in a more sophisticated way.

How Many Typefaces to Use?

You don't need to use several typefaces to create a great design. A single classic typeface may be all you need. Simply play with formatting and use contrasts. If you use too many typefaces, you will end up with a confusing and distracting result. Moreover, it will look unprofessional. In general, when in doubt, stick with only one classic typeface.

If you think that one typeface is not enough for your design, don't use more than 3 typefaces. And only one of them can be fancy or decorative. The others must be clean and simple.

Remember the three main font pairing principles I explained you previously. The fonts must be appropriate to your target audience and communicate the emotions and message you want your design to arise.

Main Principles of Perfecting Your Typefaces

Creating perfect typography is important for every design. Don't ignore this piece of design process. In this chapter, you will learn about three simple secrets to make sure your typography always looks perfect. Use them to make your design look professional and sophisticated.

Kerning

Kerning refers to the process of adjusting the space *between two characters*: letter, punctuation, numbers, etc. Usually, it is applied to logos and big titles with the size higher than 20 points. Sometimes, a font's default kerning doesn't look well when certain letter combinations are used. In these cases, you'll want to manually adjust it so the spacing between all the letters looks equal. It doesn't need to be mathematically equal though, but only to create optical illusion that spacing is equal. It's because each letter has its own unique shape (straight-edged and rounded letters) and not always do they perfectly fit together when put in pairs.

Sometimes, a too wide gap between letters may look like a space between two words and break your text. Or two letters may be placed so close together that become unreadable. The usual examples are letters "r" and "n". If they are too close to each other, they form the letter "m". Check out these examples of bad kerning usage.

If it's hard to recognize where you need to make kerning adjustments, flip your title upside down to spot the spacing problems. This will help you to focus on the letterforms and notice which spaces need to be adjusted.

If your software doesn't provide kerning function, you will need to split your title into letters or letter groups to adjust the spacing manually. However, kerning is applied **only to big titles**. So, don't waste your time on large blocks of body text. They don't need manual kerning because any kerning problems won't be visible at small text sizes.

Moreover, kerning should be one of the last steps when creating your design. Only when the final choice regarding your font and formatting has been made, move on to kerning to refine and polish your design. In some cases, it isn't needed at all.

Tracking

Tracking refers to adjusting the spacing equally between *all the characters* in your text. Rather than adjusting only one pair of letters like with kerning, tracking applies equal spacing to *all* the letters in your chosen text at once. You can adjust spacing in a single word, a sentence, or in whole paragraphs or pages automatically by using the functionality of your image editor. If any tracking is necessary, you'll want to do that before kerning. Increasing the spacing between letters is an easy technique that helps make your title look more impressive and epic.

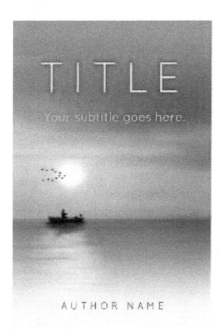

However, you should be careful with tracking, because if overused it can lead to difficulty in reading.

Leading

Leading (pronounced "ledding") is the spacing between lines of your text. You already use this setting in your text-editing program every time your text is started in a new row. This is a very simple principle that determines how text is spaced vertically in lines.

If your title has multiple lines of text, you'll want to make sure there is an appropriate distance between them to make your title readable. If the space is too high or too narrow, you will need to reduce it manually. If your image editor app doesn't provide this function, you will need to create two or three separate title lines and then place them in appropriate distance manually.

Whether you're designing a social media post or a Christmas greeting card, it's worth knowing these basic typography concepts and how to apply them to your designs. Kerning, Tracking and Leading are important in typography and should not be ignored. It is the finishing touch on your designs that makes everything easily readable and professionally looking. Consider these techniques before completing every design. However, it doesn't mean that you always need to apply them. Not always they are necessary.

10 Resources to Download Free Fonts

As we already discussed before, choosing a typeface is an important part of the design process. One of the main goals of the typeface is to communicate your message and mood and evoke emotions in the reader. The bad news is that the selection of standard fonts that are available on your computer is limited. The good news is that you can add new fonts to your computer easily and free of charge. There is really a wide variety of free fonts available in different resources. I have listed some of them below. However, there is a ton of paid fonts, too. So, if you don't find what you are looking for in free resources, then look for paid fonts. Simply search for them on Google.

1. Google Fonts – search by numerous font categories and choose exactly what you like.
2. Dafont – browse fonts by alphabetical listing, by style, by author or by popularity.
3. 1001 Free Fonts – Graffiti, Helloween, Gothic, Fantasy – these are just a few of fancy fonts categories you can choose from. Check them out!
4. Font Space – a collection of over 31,000 free fonts shared by designers around the world.
5. Fontsquirrel – hand-selected typefaces that are presented in an easy-to-use format.
6. Urban Fonts – nearly 8,000 free fonts to choose from.
7. Font Zone – thousands of free fonts to enhance your own websites, documents, greeting cards, and more. You can browse popular fonts by themes, name or style.
8. Font Bundles – beautiful and stylish fonts that you can get for free.
9. Behance – huge selection of stylish fonts. Pay with a Tweet and get any of them.
10. Ffonts – choose from 14, 000 fonts and use them as you wish.

If you want to learn about other free tools that you can use for creating visuals, get this book: "100+ Free Tools to Create Visuals for Web & Social Media". You can download it for free from my webpage.

Typeface Licenses Explained

Similarly like with photos and vector files, you need to make sure you are allowed to use the typefaces downloaded from the Internet. Including the web pages I listed before. Typefaces are considered as software and they should be treated like any other software license. Many free fonts are licensed for personal use only and do not include a commercial license. It may also happen that the license prohibits you from using the font in certain commercial works like in a logo but allow you to use it for other purposes. So, always check out the license terms before you use the font for your design.

If you use unlicensed font, it may happen that you will not be able to embed it in your pdf file, which is necessary to make sure that your fonts will look the same when the file is opened on other computers. Moreover, it's an intellectual property violation. There are cases when design agencies have been sued for using unlicensed fonts.

How to Install New Typefaces on Your Computer?

In case you are wondering how to technically add a new font to your computer, it's actually very easy. So, don't be afraid. You don't need to be a tech geek or a designer to do that. Just go to any website that I listed before, choose the font you like and download it. Watch this video tutorial. And remember to read the license terms of each font to make sure you can use them for commercial use.

What Software and Apps to Use for Creating Your Designs?

There are many software and apps you can use for creating your designs. Your choice mainly depends on your skills and abilities. If you are skillful in Photoshop, Adobe Illustrator or Corel Draw, use them. The disadvantage of these software is that they are rather expensive. If you are not going to use them professionally, most probably it's not worth investing in them.

Instead, you can choose from these tools listed below. Most of them are free.

1. GIMP – this free software has rather similar functionality to Photoshop, which means that it works the best for picture (bitmap) retouching and editing. If you don't know how to use it, search for video tutorials on YouTube.

2. Inkscape – this software has similar functionality to Adobe Illustrator and CorelDraw. It is used for creating or editing vector graphics such as illustrations, diagrams, line arts, charts, logos and others. If you don't know how to use it, you will need to spend some time learning it first.

3. PowerPoint – the easiest software to use and won't cost you a dime if you already have it on your computer. If you don't, you can use its free trial version or subscribe for all MS Office products just for $7.99/month. You can use PowerPoint for creating vector graphics and also for doing simple photo editing. If you want to learn more about PowerPoint functionality, check out my tutorials on YouTube.

4. Canva – online app that offers many easily editable templates to choose from. All you need to do is drag and drop the elements of your design, change colors and fonts.

5. Pixlr–free online app that is an alternative to Photoshop and Gimp. The advantage is you don't need to install it. Good for photo editing and working with picture layers.

If you want to learn about other free tools that you can use for creating visuals, get this book: "100+ Free Tools to Create Visuals for Web & Social Media". You can download it for free from my webpage.

Use Free Images - <u>10 Free Resources</u>

A single picture can be worth a thousand words. But, where to find free images for your website design, blog, Facebook or Twitter post, or for a small business ad design without spending a lot of money for it? Of course, if the budget allows it, you can buy such images on websites like istock.com, shutterstock.com or any other similar sites. If you know how to, you can create images by yourself. However, quality pictures can also be found online for free – without investing much work into creating them, and at the same time not infringing any copyrights.

There are many portals on the Internet that offer free quality photos. Some of the authors ask for attribution, some of them allow using their pictures only for personal use, but there are also plenty of those who allow using their photos and images for commercial use. Some restrictions may apply; therefore you should always check the license terms first, but you can mostly use these pictures for your blog posts, website and social networks, free of charge.

1.<u>Free Images</u> – More than 388 000 free photos and illustrations.
2. <u>Pixabay</u> – More than 310 000 pictures – photos, vectors, and artistic illustrations. You can use every single one of them, both in digital and printed format, including commercial use. Many of the images used in this book come from this portal.
3. <u>Snapwire Snaps</u> – free photos from 200,177 of the world's top photographers.
4. <u>tookapic</u> – high quality free and premium 13,846 stock photos.
5. <u>Public Domain Photos</u> – 5 000 free photos and 8000 cliparts which can be used as you wish – even for commercial purposes.
6. <u>Free Photos Bank</u> – wide variety of different photos – from cables to toys and office supplies.
7. <u>Picjumbo</u> – simple navigation and a huge image library. Many beautiful pictures of food and drinks, which might be very useful for marketing a restaurant or a bar.
8. <u>FancyCrave</u> – high-resolution food, nature, people, architecture and other photos from professional photographers.
9. <u>FreeJPG</u> – great source of technology, people, texture, travel, religion and other images – more than 10 000 images.
10. <u>Good Free Photos</u> – a gallery of thousands of unique and free public domain stock photos. Categorized by location for travel photos, species for animal and plant photos, and types of objects for other photos.

Conclusion

Congratulations! Thank you very much for reading all the way to the end. You've made it through the book and now have a better understanding of how to create great and effective visuals for your website, social media, advertising, business cards and other projects. Hopefully, you have got some tips and insights from this book that will stick with you forever. Even it was only one helpful tip it may create a big difference in your future graphic design projects.

www.ingramcontent.com/pod-product-compliance
Lightning Source LLC
Chambersburg PA
CBHW082122070326
40690CB00049B/4158

9 781803 627335